touchably textured
Baby Afghans

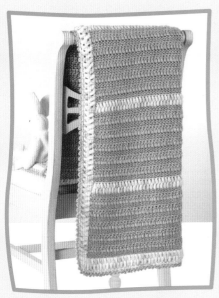

These five soft baby blankets are such a delight to crochet! Each offers a uniquely textured pattern created by braids, clusters, or puff stitches. Special details such as a lacy edging or an unexpected row of contrasting color give extra interest to these mostly easy afghans. Four of the designs use light or medium weight yarn, while one uses both. Whether you want to fashion a blanket for a new family member or need a gift for a baby shower, these cozy designs will be warmly received!

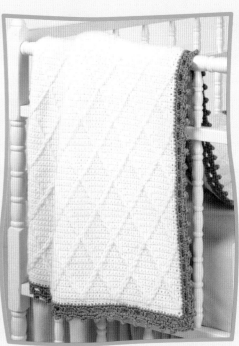

LEISURE ARTS, INC.
Little Rock, Arkansas

rainbow puffs

Shown on front cover.

◼◼◻◻ EASY +

Finished Size: 35" x 49" (89 cm x 124.5 cm)

MATERIALS

Light Weight Yarn **3** LIGHT
[5 ounces, 468 yards
(140 grams, 429 meters) per skein]:
    MC (Pink) - 4 skeins
[4.25 ounces, 333 yards
(120 grams, 304 meters) per skein]:
    CC (Variegated) - 1 skein
Crochet hook, size G (4 mm) **or** size
    needed for gauge

GAUGE: In pattern, (sc, ch 1) 11 times
    and Rows 1-15 = 4" (10 cm)

Gauge Swatch: 4¼" (10.75 cm) square
With MC, ch 24.
Rows 1-16: Work same as Body: 2 dc,
11 Clusters, and 12 ch-1 sps.
Finish off.

STITCH GUIDE

CLUSTER (uses one ch-1 sp)
★ YO, insert hook in ch-1 sp indicated, YO
and pull up a loop, YO and draw through
2 loops on hook; repeat from ★ once **more**,
YO and draw through all 3 loops on hook.
PUFF ST (uses one sp)
★ YO, insert hook in sp indicated, YO and
pull up a loop; repeat from ★ 2 times **more**,
YO and draw through all 7 loops on hook.

BODY

With MC, ch 174; place marker in second ch
from hook to mark Edging placement.

Row 1 (Right side): Sc in second ch from hook,
★ ch 1, skip next ch, sc in next ch; repeat from
★ across: 87 sc and 86 chs.

Note: Loop a short piece of yarn around any
stitch to mark Row 1 as **right** side.

Rows 2 and 3: Ch 1, turn; sc in first sc, ★ ch 1,
skip next ch, sc in next sc; repeat from ★ across:
87 sc and 86 ch-1 sps.

Row 4: Ch 4 **(counts as first dc plus ch 1)**, turn;
(work Cluster in next ch-1 sp, ch 1) across to
last sc, dc in last sc: 2 dc, 86 Clusters, and
87 ch-1 sps.

Row 5: Ch 1, turn; sc in first dc, ch 1, skip next
ch-1 sp and next Cluster, ★ sc in next ch-1 sp,
ch 1, skip next Cluster; repeat from ★ across
to last ch-1 sp, skip last ch-1 sp, sc in last dc:
87 sc and 86 chs.

Rows 6 and 7: Ch 1, turn; sc in first sc, ★ ch 1,
skip next ch, sc in next sc; repeat from ★ across:
87 sc and 86 ch-1 sps.

Rows 8-23: Repeat Rows 4-7, 4 times; at end of
Row 23, finish off.

Row 24: With **wrong** side facing, join CC with
hdc in first sc *(see Joining With Hdc, page 16)*;
(work Puff St in next ch-1 sp, ch 1) across to
last sc, hdc in last sc: 2 hdc, 86 Puff Sts, and
86 ch-1 sps.

Row 25: Ch 2 **(counts as first hdc)**, turn; work Puff St in next ch-1 sp, ch 1, ★ skip next Puff St, work Puff St in next ch-1 sp, ch 1; repeat from ★ across to last Puff St, skip last Puff St, hdc in last hdc; finish off.

Row 26: With **right** side facing, join MC with sc in first hdc **(see Joining With Sc, page 16)**; ch 1, skip next Puff St, ★ sc in next ch-1 sp, ch 1, skip next Puff St; repeat from ★ across to last ch-1 sp, skip last ch-1 sp, sc in last hdc: 87 sc and 86 chs.

Rows 27-173: Repeat Rows 2-26, 5 times; then repeat Rows 2-23 once **more**.

EDGING

Rnd 1: With **right** side facing, join CC with sc in first sc; ch 2, sc in same st, ch 1, skip next ch, (sc in next sc, ch 1, skip next ch) across to last sc, (sc, ch 2, sc) in last sc, ch 1; † working in end of rows, skip first sc row, sc in next sc row, ch 1, skip next sc row, sc in next dc row, ch 1, sc in next sc row, ch 1, skip next sc row, sc in next sc row, ch 1, [sc in next dc row, ch 1, skip next sc row, sc in next sc row, ch 1, skip next sc row, sc in next dc row, ch 1, sc in next sc row, ch 1, skip next sc row, sc in next sc row, ch 1] twice, ★ sc in next hdc row, ch 1, skip next hdc row, sc in next sc row, ch 1, skip next sc row, sc in next sc row, ch 1, sc in next dc row, ch 1, skip next sc row, sc in next sc row, ch 1, skip next sc row, [sc in next dc row, ch 1, sc in next sc row, ch 1, skip next sc row, sc in next sc row, ch 1, sc in next dc row, ch 1, skip next sc row, sc in next sc row, ch 1, skip next sc row] twice; repeat from ★ 5 times **more** †; working in free loops of beginning ch **(Fig. 1, page 16)**, (sc, ch 2, sc) in first ch, ch 1, skip next ch, (sc in next ch, ch 1, skip next ch) across to marked ch, (sc, ch 2, sc) in marked ch, ch 1; repeat from † to † once; join with slip st to first sc: 386 sc and 386 sps.

Rnd 2: Do **not** turn; keeping loop on the hook **loose**, work (Puff St, ch 2, Puff St) in next ch-2 sp, ch 1, ★ (work Puff St in next ch-1 sp, ch 1) across to next corner ch-2 sp, work (Puff St, ch 2, Puff St) in corner sp, ch 1; repeat from ★ 2 times **more**, (work Puff St in next ch-1 sp, ch 1) across; join with slip st to top of first Puff St.

Rnd 3: Turn; slip st in next ch-1 sp, keeping loop on the hook **loose**, work Puff St in same sp, ch 1, ★ (work Puff St in next ch-1 sp, ch 1) across to next corner ch-2 sp, work (Puff St, ch 2, Puff St) in corner sp, ch 1; repeat from ★ around; join with slip st to top of first Puff St.

Rnd 4: Slip st in next ch-1 sp, ch 3 **(counts as first hdc plus ch 1)**, turn; hdc in next ch-1 sp, ch 1, (hdc, ch 1) 3 times in next corner ch-2 sp, ★ (hdc in next ch-1 sp, ch 1) across to next corner ch-2 sp, (hdc, ch 1) 3 times in corner sp; repeat from ★ 2 times **more**, (hdc in next ch-1 sp, ch 1) across; join with slip st to first hdc, finish off.

Rnd 5: With **wrong** side facing, join MC with sc in any ch-1 sp; ch 3, slip st in top of sc just made, ★ sc in next ch-1 sp, ch 3, slip st in top of sc just made; repeat from ★ around; join with slip st to first sc, finish off.

summer fresh

Shown on page 4.

◖◖◻◻ **EASY**

Finished Size: 35" x 46" (89 cm x 117 cm)

MATERIALS

Medium Weight Yarn **4** **MEDIUM**
[6 ounces, 315 yards
(170 grams, 288 meters) per skein]:
  6 skeins
Crochet hook, size G (4 mm) **or** size
  needed for gauge

GAUGE: In pattern (Rows 1-11),
        17 sts and 11 rows = 4" (10 cm)

Gauge Swatch: 4¹/₂"w x 4"h (11.5 cm x 10 cm)
Ch 21.
Rows 1-11: Work same as Body: 19 sc.
Finish off.

STITCH GUIDE

CLUSTER (uses one st)
★ YO, insert hook in st indicated, YO and
pull up a loop, YO and draw through 2 loops
on hook; repeat from ★ once **more**, YO and
draw through all 3 loops on hook.
DECREASE (uses next 3 sts)
★ YO, insert hook in **next** st, YO and pull
up a loop, YO and draw through 2 loops on
hook; repeat from ★ 2 times **more**, YO and
draw through all 4 loops on hook.
ENDING DECREASE (uses last 2 sts)
★ YO, insert hook in **next** st, YO and pull
up a loop, YO and draw through 2 loops on
hook; repeat from ★ once **more**, YO and draw
through all 3 loops on hook.

BODY
Ch 141.

Row 1 (Right side)**:** Dc in fourth ch from hook
(3 skipped chs count as first dc) and in each ch
across: 139 dc.

Row 2: Ch 2 **(counts as first hdc, now and
throughout)**, turn; hdc in next dc and in each dc
across.

Row 3: Ch 3 **(counts as first dc, now and
throughout)**, turn; dc in next st, ch 3, work
Cluster in top of dc just made, ★ decrease,
ch 3, work Cluster in top of decrease just made;
repeat from ★ across to last 2 sts, work ending
decrease: 46 Clusters, 46 decreases, and 2 dc.

Row 4: Ch 3, turn; dc in same st, skip next
Cluster, (3 dc in next decrease, skip next
Cluster) across to last 2 dc, skip next dc, 2 dc in
last dc: 139 dc.

Row 5: Ch 2, turn; hdc in next dc and in each
dc across.

Row 6: Ch 3, turn; dc in next hdc and in each
hdc across.

Row 7: Ch 1, turn; sc in each dc across.

Row 8: Turn; slip st in first sc, (dc in next sc,
slip st in next sc) across: 70 slip sts and 69 dc.

Row 9: Ch 1, turn; sc in first 2 sts, ch 1, ★ skip
next slip st, sc in next dc, ch 1; repeat from ★
across to last 3 sts, skip next slip st, sc in last
2 sts: 71 sc and 68 ch-1 sps.

Row 10: Ch 1, turn; sc in each sc and in each ch-1 sp across.

Row 11: Ch 1, turn; sc in each sc across.

Rows 12-14: Repeat Rows 8-10.

Row 15: Ch 3, turn; dc in next sc and in each sc across.

Rows 16-21: Repeat Rows 2-7.

Row 22: Turn; slip st in first sc, (hdc in next sc, slip st in next sc) across: 70 slip sts and 69 hdc.

Row 23: Ch 1, turn; sc in each st across: 139 sc.

Rows 24-155: Repeat Rows 22 and 23, 66 times: 139 sc.

Row 156: Ch 3, turn; dc in next sc and in each sc across.

Row 157: Ch 2, turn; hdc in next dc and in each dc across.

Row 158: Ch 1, turn; sc in each hdc across.

Rows 159-176: Repeat Rows 3-20; at end of Row 176, do **not** finish off.

EDGING

Rnd 1: Ch 1, turn; 2 sc in first dc, skip next dc, sc in next 136 dc, 3 sc in last dc; work 184 sc evenly spaced across end of rows to beginning ch; working in free loops of beginning ch *(Fig. 1, page 16)*, 3 sc in first ch, skip next ch, sc in next 136 chs, 3 sc in next ch; work 184 sc evenly spaced across end of rows, sc in same st as first sc; join with slip st to first sc: 652 sc.

Rnd 2: Ch 2, 2 hdc in same st as joining, ★ hdc in next sc and in each sc across to center sc of next corner 3-sc group, 3 hdc in center sc; repeat from ★ 2 times **more**, hdc in next sc and in each sc across; join with slip st to first hdc: 660 hdc.

Rnd 3: Ch 2, dc in same st as joining **(beginning Cluster made)**, ch 3, work Cluster in third ch from hook, (work Cluster in next hdc, ch 3, work Cluster in third ch from hook) twice, ★ (decrease, ch 3, work Cluster in third ch from hook) across to next corner 3-hdc group, (work Cluster in next hdc, ch 3, work Cluster in third ch from hook) 3 times; repeat from ★ 2 times **more**, (decrease, ch 3, work Cluster in third ch from hook) across; skip first hdc and join with slip st to next dc, finish off.

Shown on page 5.
◼◼◻◻ **EASY +**

Finished Size: 33¹/₂" x 41¹/₂"
(85 cm x 105.5 cm)

MATERIALS
Light Weight Yarn **LIGHT 3**
[5 ounces, 468 yards
(140 grams, 429 meters) per skein]:
    MC (White) - 4 skeins
Medium Weight Yarn **MEDIUM 4**
[6 ounces, 312 yards
(170 grams, 285 meters) per skein]:
    CC (Lavender) - 1 skein
Crochet hooks, sizes F (3.75 mm) **and**
    G (4 mm) **or** sizes needed for gauge
Safety pins - 49

GAUGE: With larger size hook, in pattern,
        22 sts and 28 rows = 5" (12.75 cm)

Gauge Swatch: 4¹/₂"w x 3"h (11.5 cm x 7.5 cm)
With larger size hook and MC, ch 21.
Rows 1-16: Work same as Body: 20 sts.
Finish off.

STITCH GUIDE
LOOP ST (uses one sc)
Insert hook in sc indicated, wrap yarn around index finger of left hand once **more**, insert hook through all loops on finger following direction indicated by arrow **(Fig. A)**, being careful to hook all loops **(Fig. B)**, draw through st, remove finger from loop, YO and draw through all 3 loops on hook pulling loop to measure approximately ¹/₂" (12 mm) **(Loop St made, Fig. C)**.

Fig. A

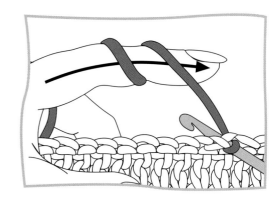

Fig. B   **Fig. C**

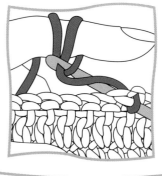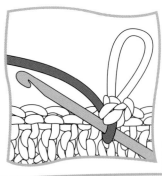

BODY
With larger size hook and MC, ch 141.

Row 1 (Right side): Sc in second ch from hook and in each ch across: 140 sc.

Note: Loop a short piece of yarn around any stitch to mark Row 1 as **right** side.

Row 2: Ch 1, turn; work Loop St in first sc, sc in next 8 sc, (work Loop St in next 2 sc, sc in next 8 sc) across to last sc, work Loop St in last sc.

Row 3 AND ALL RIGHT SIDE ROWS: Ch 1, turn; sc in each st across, keeping loops to toward you.

Row 4: Ch 1, turn; work Loop St in first sc, sc in next 8 sc, (work Loop St in next 2 sc, sc in next 8 sc) across to last sc, work Loop St in last sc.

Row 6: Ch 1, turn; sc in first sc, work Loop St in next sc, sc in next 6 sc, work Loop St in next sc, ★ sc in next 2 sc, work Loop St in next sc, sc in next 6 sc, work Loop St in next sc; repeat from ★ across to last sc, sc in last sc.

Row 8: Ch 1, turn; sc in first 2 sc, work Loop St in next sc, (sc in next 4 sc, work Loop St in next sc) across to last 2 sc, sc in last 2 sc.

Row 10: Ch 1, turn; sc in first 3 sc, work Loop St in next sc, sc in next 2 sc, work Loop St in next sc, ★ sc in next 6 sc, work Loop St in next sc, sc in next 2 sc, work Loop St in next sc; repeat from ★ across to last 3 sc, sc in last 3 sc.

Rows 12 and 14: Ch 1, turn; sc in first 4 sc, work Loop St in next 2 sc, (sc in next 8 sc, work Loop St in next 2 sc) across to last 4 sc, sc in last 4 sc.

Row 16: Ch 1, turn; sc in first 3 sc, work Loop St in next sc, sc in next 2 sc, work Loop St in next sc, ★ sc in next 6 sc, work Loop St in next sc, sc in next 2 sc, work Loop St in next sc; repeat from ★ across to last 3 sc, sc in last 3 sc.

Row 18: Ch 1, turn; sc in first 2 sc, work Loop St in next sc, (sc in next 4 sc, work Loop St in next sc) across to last 2 sc, sc in last 2 sc.

Row 20: Ch 1, turn; sc in first sc, work Loop St in next sc, sc in next 6 sc, work Loop St in next sc, ★ sc in next 2 sc, work Loop St in next sc, sc in next 6 sc, work Loop St in next sc; repeat from ★ across to last sc, sc in last sc.

Row 22: Ch 1, turn; work Loop St in first sc, sc in next 8 sc, (work Loop St in next 2 sc, sc in next 8 sc) across to last sc, work Loop St in last sc.

Rows 23-223: Repeat Rows 3-22, 10 times; then repeat Row 3 once **more**; do **not** cut yarn.

Place loop from hook onto a safety pin to keep piece from unraveling while braiding loops.

With **right** side facing and beginning in bottom right corner, insert hook in first loop; working **diagonally to the left**, (hook next loop and pull through loop on hook) until you run out of loops at the edge of the piece; secure last loop with a safety pin. Repeat until all left diagonal loops have been "chained up" and secured with safety pins (when there are 2 loops side-by-side, begin the left diagonal braid with the loop to the right).

Repeat these instructions diagonally to the right until all right diagonal loops have been "chained up" and secured with safety pins.

Joining Rnd: With **right** side facing, place loop with working yarn onto larger size hook, ch 1; working in end of rows **and** through safety pinned loop when you reach one, work 176 sc evenly spaced across; working in free loops of beginning ch **(Fig. 1, page 16)**, 3 sc in first ch, work 136 sc evenly spaced across to ch at base of last sc, 3 sc in ch; working in end of rows **and** through safety pinned loop when you reach one, work 176 sc evenly spaced across; working in sts across last row **and** through safety pinned loop when you reach one, 3 sc in first sc, work 136 sc evenly spaced across to last sc, 3 sc in last sc; join with slip st to first sc, finish off: 636 sc.

Instructions continued on page 12.

EDGING

Rnd 1: With **right** side facing and using smaller size hook, join CC with sc in center sc of any corner 3-sc group *(see Joining With Sc, page 16)*; sc in same st and in each sc across to center sc of next corner 3-sc group, 3 sc in center sc, ★ sc in next sc and in each sc across to center sc of next corner 3-sc group, 3 sc in center sc; repeat from ★ once **more**, sc in next sc and in each sc across, sc in same st as first sc; join with slip st to first sc: 644 sc.

Rnd 2: Ch 2 **(counts as first hdc)**, 2 hdc in same st as joining, ★ † hdc in next sc, ch 2, (skip next 2 sc, hdc in next 2 sc, ch 2) across to within 2 sts of next corner 3-sc group, skip next 2 sc, hdc in next sc †, 3 hdc in next sc; repeat from ★ 2 times **more**, then repeat from † to † once; join with slip st to first hdc: 332 hdc and 160 ch-2 sps.

To work Picot, ch 3, slip st in top of sc just made.

Rnd 3: Ch 1, sc in same st as joining, work Picot, 2 sc in next corner hdc, work Picot, sc in next 2 hdc, ★ † (sc, work Picot, sc) in next ch-2 sp, sc in next 2 hdc †; repeat from † to † across to center hdc of next corner 3-hdc group, 2 sc in corner hdc, work Picot, sc in next 2 hdc; repeat from ★ 2 times **more**, then repeat from † to † across to last ch-2 sp, (sc, work Picot, sc) in last ch-2 sp, sc in last hdc; join with slip st to first sc, finish off.

kissed by sunshine

Shown on page 8.

◖■■□□◗ EASY +

Finished Size: 33" x 42½" (84 cm x 108 cm)

MATERIALS
Light Weight Yarn (3 LIGHT)
[5 ounces, 468 yards
(140 grams, 429 meters) per skein]:
    MC (Green) - 5 skeins
    CC (Yellow) - 1 skein
Crochet hook, size F (3.75 mm) **or** size needed for gauge

GAUGE: In pattern, 20 sts = 4" (10 cm);
            12 rows = 3¾" (9.5 cm)

Gauge Swatch: 4"w x 3"h (10 cm x 7.5 cm)
With MC, ch 21.
Rows 1-10: Work same as Body: 20 sc.
Finish off.

STITCH GUIDE

CLUSTER (uses one dc)
YO, insert hook from **front** to **back** around post of dc just made *(Fig. 2, page 16)*, YO and pull up a loop, YO and draw through 2 loops on hook (2 loops remaining on hook), YO, insert hook from **front** to **back** around post of **same** dc, YO and pull up a loop, YO and draw through all 4 loops on hook.

BODY

With MC, ch 161.

Row 1: Sc in second ch from hook and in each ch across: 160 sc.

Row 2 (Right side): Ch 1, turn; sc in each sc across.

Note: Loop a short piece of yarn around any stitch to mark Row 2 as **right** side.

Row 3: Ch 3 **(counts as first dc, now and throughout)**, turn; dc in next sc, work Cluster, ★ skip next sc, dc in next sc, work Cluster; repeat from ★ across to last 2 sc, skip next sc, dc in last sc: 79 Clusters and 81 dc.

Row 4: Ch 1, turn; sc in each st across: 160 sc.

Rows 5-22: Repeat Rows 3 and 4, 9 times; at end of last row, finish off.

Row 23: With **wrong** side facing, join CC with sc in first sc *(see Joining With Sc, page 16)*; sc in next sc and in each sc across.

Row 24: Ch 1, turn; sc in each sc across; finish off.

Row 25: With **wrong** side facing, join MC with dc in first sc *(see Joining With Dc, page 16)*; dc in next sc, work Cluster, ★ skip next sc, dc in next sc, work Cluster; repeat from ★ across to last 2 sc, skip next sc, dc in last sc: 79 Clusters and 81 dc.

Row 26: Ch 1, turn; sc in each st across: 160 sc.

Rows 27-131: Repeat Rows 5-26, 4 times; then repeat Rows 5-21 once **more:** 79 Clusters and 81 dc.

Rows 132 and 133: Ch 1, turn; sc in each st across: 160 sc.

Finish off.

EDGING

Rnd 1: With **right** side facing, join CC with sc in first sc on Row 133; sc in same st and in each sc across to last sc, 3 sc in last sc; work 204 sc evenly spaced across end of rows to beginning ch; working in free loops of beginning ch *(Fig. 1, page 16)*, 3 sc in ch at base of first sc, sc in each ch across to last ch, 3 sc in last ch; work 204 sc evenly spaced across end of rows, sc in same st as first sc; join with slip st to first sc: 736 sc.

Rnd 2: Ch 3, hdc in third ch from hook, sc in same st as joining, ★ † slip st in next sc, ch 3, hdc in third ch from hook, sc in next sc †; repeat from † to † across to center sc of next corner 3-sc group, (slip st, ch 3, hdc in third ch from hook, sc) in corner sc; repeat from ★ 2 times **more**, then repeat from † to † across; join with slip st to st at base of beginning ch-3, finish off.

cloud-soft comfort

Shown on page 9.
◼◼◻◻ **EASY**

Finished Size: 38" x 43" (96.5 cm x 109 cm)

MATERIALS

Light Weight Yarn 🌀 **LIGHT 3**
[6 ounces, 430 yards
(170 grams, 393 meters) per skein]:
    4 skeins
Crochet hook, size F (3.75 mm) **or** size
    needed for gauge

GAUGE: In pattern,
        20 sts and 14 rows = 4" (10 cm)

Gauge Swatch: 4³/₄"w x 4"h (12 cm x 10 cm)
Ch 24.
Rows 1-14: Work same as Body: 18 dc and
5 Puff Sts.
Finish off.

STITCH GUIDE

TREBLE CROCHET *(abbreviated tr)*
YO twice, insert hook in sc indicated, YO
and pull up a loop (4 loops on hook), (YO
and draw through 2 loops on hook) 3 times.
PUFF ST (uses one sc)
★ YO, insert hook in sc indicated, YO and
pull up a loop; repeat from ★ 3 times **more**,
YO and draw through all 9 loops on hook.
CROSS ST (uses 2 sc)
Tr in next sc, working **behind** tr just made, tr
in sc **before** sc just worked into.
DOUBLE CROSS ST (uses next 4 sc)
Skip next 2 sc, tr in next 2 sc, working
behind 2-tr group just made, tr in each
skipped sc.

BODY
Ch 184.

Row 1 (Right side)**:** Sc in second ch from hook
and in each ch across: 183 sc.

Row 2: Ch 3 **(counts as first dc, now and
throughout)**, turn; work Puff St in next sc, ★ skip
next sc, dc in next 3 sc, working around 3-dc
group just made, dc in skipped sc, work Puff St
in next sc; repeat from ★ across to last sc, dc in
last sc: 146 dc and 37 Puff Sts.

Row 3: Ch 1, turn; sc in each st across: 183 sc.

Repeat Rows 2 and 3 until Body measures
approximately 41" (104 cm) from beginning ch,
ending by working Row 3; do **not** finish off.

EDGING

Rnd 1: Ch 1, do **not** turn; 2 sc in last sc made
on last row of Body; work 203 sc evenly spaced
across end of rows; working in free loops of
beginning ch *(Fig. 1, page 16)*, 3 sc in first ch,
work 179 sc evenly spaced across to ch at base
of last sc, 3 sc in ch; work 203 sc evenly spaced
across end of rows; working in sts across last
row, 3 sc in first sc, work 179 sc evenly spaced
across, sc in same st as first sc; join with slip st
to first sc: 776 sc.

Rnd 2: Ch 4 (counts as first tr), working behind tr just made, tr in last sc worked on Rnd 1, work Cross St twice, skip next sc, tr in next 2 sc, working behind 2-tr group just made, tr in sc before skipped sc and in skipped sc, ★ work Double Cross Sts across to center sc of next corner 3-sc group, work Cross St 3 times, skip next sc, tr in next 2 sc, working behind 2-tr group just made, tr in sc before skipped sc and in next skipped sc; repeat from ★ 2 times more, work Double Cross Sts across working second tr of last Double Cross St in same sc as second tr worked on this rnd; join with slip st to first tr.

Rnd 3: Ch 1, sc in same st as joining and in each st around; join with slip st to first sc, finish off.

general instructions

ABBREVIATIONS

CC	Contrasting Color
ch(s)	chain(s)
cm	centimeters
dc	double crochet(s)
hdc	half double crochet(s)
MC	Main Color
mm	millimeters
Rnd(s)	Round(s)
sc	single crochet(s)
sp(s)	space(s)
st(s)	stitch(es)
tr	treble crochet(s)
YO	yarn over

★ — work instructions following ★ as many more times as indicated in addition to the first time.

† to † — work all instructions from first † to second † as many times as specified.

( ) or [ ] — work enclosed instructions as many times as specified by the number immediately following or work all enclosed instructions in the stitch or space indicated or contains explanatory remarks.

colon (:) — the number(s) given after a colon at the end of a row or round denote(s) the number of stitches or spaces you should have on that row or round.

GAUGE

Exact gauge is essential for proper size. Before beginning your project, make the sample swatch given in the individual instruction in the yarn and hook specified. After completing the swatch, measure it, counting your stitches and rows carefully. If your swatch is larger or smaller than specified, make another, changing hook size to get the correct gauge. Keep trying until you find the size hook that will give you the specified gauge.

Yarn Weight Symbol & Names	LACE 0	SUPER FINE 1	FINE 2	LIGHT 3	MEDIUM 4	BULKY 5	SUPER BULKY 6
Type of Yarns in Category	Fingering, 10-count crochet thread	Sock, Fingering Baby	Sport, Baby	DK, Light Worsted	Worsted, Afghan, Aran	Chunky, Craft, Rug	Bulky, Roving
Crochet Gauge* Ranges in Single Crochet to 4" (10 cm)	32-42 double crochets**	21-32 sts	16-20 sts	12-17 sts	11-14 sts	8-11 sts	5-9 sts
Advised Hook Size Range	Steel*** 6,7,8 Regular hook B-1	B-1 to E-4	E-4 to 7	7 to I-9	I-9 to K-10.5	K-10.5 to M-13	M-13 and larger

*GUIDELINES ONLY: The chart above reflects the most commonly used gauges and hook sizes for specific yarn categories.

** Lace weight yarns are usually crocheted on larger-size hooks to create lacy openwork patterns. Accordingly, a gauge range is difficult to determine. Always follow the gauge stated in your pattern.

*** Steel crochet hooks are sized differently from regular hooks–the higher the number the smaller the hook, which is the reverse of regular hook sizing.

CROCHET HOOKS													
U.S.	B-1	C-2	D-3	E-4	F-5	G-6	H-8	I-9	J-10	K-10½	N	P	Q
Metric - mm	2.25	2.75	3.25	3.5	3.75	4	5	5.5	6	6.5	9	10	15

◼☐☐☐ BEGINNER	Projects for first-time crocheters using basic stitches. Minimal shaping.
◼◼☐☐ EASY	Projects using yarn with basic stitches, repetitive stitch patterns, simple color changes, and simple shaping and finishing.
◼◼◼☐ INTERMEDIATE	Projects using a variety of techniques, such as basic lace patterns or color patterns, mid-level shaping and finishing.
◼◼◼◼ EXPERIENCED	Projects with intricate stitch patterns, techniques and dimension, such as non-repeating patterns, multi-color techniques, fine threads, small hooks, detailed shaping and refined finishing.

CROCHET TERMINOLOGY		
UNITED STATES		INTERNATIONAL
slip stitch (slip st)	=	single crochet (sc)
single crochet (sc)	=	double crochet (dc)
half double crochet (hdc)	=	half treble crochet (htr)
double crochet (dc)	=	treble crochet(tr)
treble crochet (tr)	=	double treble crochet (dtr)
double treble crochet (dtr)	=	triple treble crochet (ttr)
triple treble crochet (tr tr)	=	quadruple treble crochet (qtr)
skip	=	miss

JOINING WITH SC

When instructed to join with a sc, begin with a slip knot on the hook. Insert the hook in the stitch or space indicated, YO and pull up a loop, YO and draw through both loops on hook.

JOINING WITH HDC

When instructed to join with a hdc, begin with a slip knot on the hook. YO, holding loop on hook, insert hook in the stitch or space indicated, YO and pull up a loop, YO and draw through all 3 loops on hook.

JOINING WITH DC

When instructed to join with a dc, begin with a slip knot on the hook. YO, holding loop on hook, insert hook in stitch or space indicated, YO and pull up a loop (3 loops on hook), (YO and draw through 2 loops on hook) twice.

FREE LOOPS OF A CHAIN

When instructed to work in free loops of a chain, work in loop indicated by arrow **(Fig. 1)**.

Fig. 1

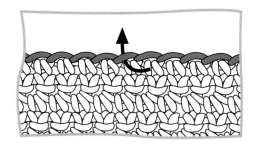

WORKING AROUND POST OF STITCH

Work around post of stitch indicated, inserting hook in direction of arrow **(Fig. 2)**.

Fig. 2

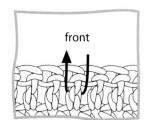

front